Sports Illustrated
SMALL BOAT
SAILING

The Sports Illustrated Library

BOOKS ON TEAM SPORTS

Baseball   Basketball   Football   Ice Hockey

BOOKS ON INDIVIDUAL SPORTS

Badminton   Golf   Skiing
Fencing   Horseback Riding   Squash
Fly Fishing   The Shotgun   Tennis
Gaited Riding   Shotgun Sports   Track and Field: Running Events

BOOKS ON WATER SPORTS

Better Boating   Junior Sailing
Diving   Small Boat Sailing   Swimming

SPECIAL BOOKS

Dog Training   Safe Driving

Sports Illustrated
SMALL BOAT
SAILING

By the Editors of
Sports Illustrated

Illustrations by
A. Ravielli and Russ Hoover

J. B. LIPPINCOTT COMPANY
Philadelphia and New York

U.S. Library of Congress Cataloging in Publication Data

Main entry under title:

Sports illustrated small boat sailing.

  (Sports illustrated library)
  First ed. published in 1960 under title: Sports illustrated
book of small boat sailing.
  1. Sailing. I. Sports illustrated (Chicago) II. Title:
Small boating sailing.
GV811.S73 1972   797.1'24   73-38684
ISBN-0-397-00861-9
ISBN-0-397-00860-0 (pbk.)

Chapters 4 and 5 are reprinted in slightly revised form from
"A New Dimension in Sailing," by Mort Lund with George
O'Day, in *Sports Illustrated*, April 3 and 24, 1961.

Photographs from *Sports Illustrated*, © Time Inc.

Cover photograph: John G. Zimmerman

Photographs on pages 18 and 70: Tom Ettinger

Photographs on pages 15, 16, 17, 18, 19, 20, 21, 22, 23, 24,
25, 26, 27, 28, 58 and 84: *Yacht Racing*

Contents

1. CLASS BOATS   11

    THE LANGUAGE OF SAILING   11
    A GLOSSARY OF NAUTICAL JARGON   12
    POINTS OF SAILING   13
    CHOOSING A CLASS   14
    SMALL BOATS: A REPRESENTATIVE SAMPLING   15

2. SAILING TO WINDWARD   29

    TUNING THE MAST   30
    THE FUNCTION OF FITTINGS   32
    THE FUNCTION OF SHAPE   35
    CONTROLLING THE ANGLE OF HEEL   36
    GOING AGAINST THE WIND   41
    POWER FROM SAILS   43
    SHAPING SAIL   46
    BALANCE OF BOAT   49
    CORRECTING WEATHER HELM   49
      CORRECTING BY BALANCING   53
      CORRECTING BY TRIMMING   54
      CORRECTING BY SHAPING THE MAINSAIL   54
    CORRECTING LEE HELM   55
    HIKING TO WINDWARD   56

3. SAILING TO LEEWARD   59

    SETTING THE SPINNAKER   59

JIBING: THE MODERN, SAFE TECHNIQUE   63
CARRYING THE SPINNAKER ACROSS THE WIND   69

4. SAILING A PLANING HULL   71
By Mort Lund with George O'Day

SPECIAL GEAR FOR PLANING   72
TAMING THE TRAPEZE   74
GETTING THE BOAT TO PLANE   78
STAYING ON A PLANE   80

5. OFF THE WIND IN A PLANING HULL   85
By Mort Lund with George O'Day

RIDING THE WAVES   85
WAVES FROM THE SIDE   88
WAVES FROM THE STERN   89
PLANING WITH A SPINNAKER   91
SAILING OUT OF A CAPSIZE   93

Text Revisions by Tom Ettinger

Sports Illustrated
SMALL BOAT
SAILING

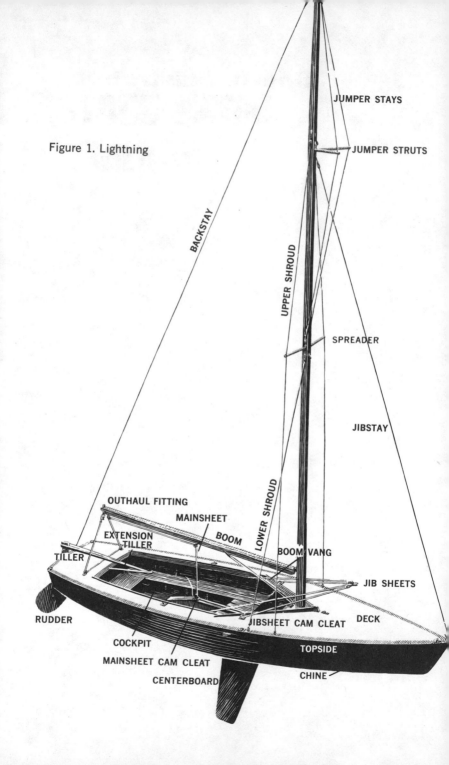

Figure 1. Lightning

1
Class
Boats

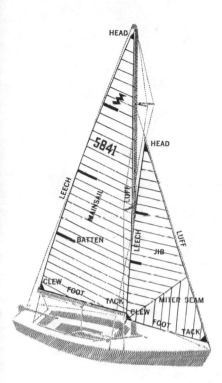

THE LANGUAGE OF SAILING

THE landlubber who goes aboard a small boat will quickly find himself exposed to a foreign language. Class boat sailing has a sizable vocabulary which sailors constantly use.

In order to prepare you for the nautical words and phrases that are used in this book, we have included not only a list of sailors' terms but also an illustration clearly showing details of a Lightning, a representative small boat, its sails, rigging, and hull, and a diagram showing the various points of sailing.

A GLOSSARY OF NAUTICAL JARGON

Abeam. Straight out from side of boat

Aft. Toward the stern, or behind it

Backwinding. When one sail throws wind onto lee side of another sail

Bearing off. Steering more to leeward, or away from the wind

Blanketing. When windward boat takes wind from leeward boat's sail

Block. Sailors' term for pulley

Boom. Horizontal pole along bottom of sail

Bow. Front of boat

Forward. Toward the bow

Halyard. Line used for raising or lowering a sail

Heading up. Steering more to windward, or toward the wind

Heeling. When a boat leans over

Knot. One nautical mile (6,080 feet) per hour

Line. General term for rope

Luffing. Shaking of sails that occurs when boat heads too much into the wind or sail is improperly trimmed

Mast. Vertical pole supporting sails

Pointing. Sailing as close into the wind as possible

Quarter. Side of boat near the stern

Reef. Lessen a sail's area by gathering in and tying down part of the sail

Running. Sailing with the wind more or less astern

Sheet. Line used in adjusting the angle of a sail to the wind

Stays. Wires from mast to deck, for support of mast

Stern. Rear end of boat

Topsides. Sides of the boat from the waterline to the deck

Trim. Adjust angle of sails to wind

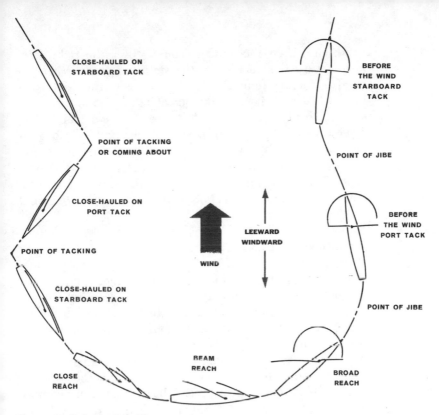

CLOSE-HAULED ON
STARBOARD TACK

BEFORE
THE WIND
STARBOARD
TACK

POINT OF TACKING
OR COMING ABOUT

POINT OF JIBE

CLOSE-HAULED ON
PORT TACK

BEFORE
THE WIND
PORT TACK

LEEWARD
WINDWARD

POINT OF TACKING

CLOSE-HAULED ON
STARBOARD TACK

WIND

POINT OF JIBE

BEAM
REACH

CLOSE
REACH

BROAD
REACH

Figure 2. Points of Sailing

POINTS OF SAILING

THOUGH a sailboat can sail a straight line away from the wind, or to *leeward*, it cannot go directly upwind (*windward*, or *to weather*). Therefore, it zigzags, or *tacks* (see Figure 2), as close as possible to the direction from which the wind is blowing, changing direction each time so that the windward side becomes the leeward side. When moving in this manner, the boat is *beating, close-hauled,* or *on the wind;* and when the wind is coming over the right (*star-board*) side, the boat is on the *starboard tack.* When the wind is coming from the left (*port*) side, the boat is on the *port tack.* A boat in the act of tacking to windward is *coming about* or *going about.* A boat in the act of tacking downwind is *jibing.* A boat can be on port or starboard tack whether it is beating, sailing a little farther away from the wind on a *close reach,* straight across the wind on a *beam reach,* still farther away from the wind on a *broad reach* or in the same direction as the wind, *before the wind.*

CHOOSING A CLASS

The process of becoming a competent sailor is not a short one but almost every minute spent in the learning is pleasant. The first step, of course, is the purchase of a boat. The purchase of a boat has, to some extent, the same excitement that attended the purchase of a car in the early days of the auto. Its color, fittings and workmanship are all subjects of endless discussion. And many thousands of families have been buying class boats, which have established standards of construction and a live market to stabilize the price. Class boats range from 11½-foot Penguins to 70-foot 12-meter boats. (A good rule is to start small and stable and go to sleek and speedy later.) The choice of class boat may well depend on the type of fleet which is the closest. The very large class boat organizations, such as those for the Lightning and the Snipe, have fleets from coast to coast. The whereabouts of the manufacturers of class boats and the location of the class secretaries can be obtained by scanning one of the boating annuals published yearly by the major yachting magazines. These annuals provide a wealth of information on all sailing craft. Also, one can learn a great deal about local sailing activities and classes by spending an afternoon at a local sailing club. Any fleet of sailors is always delighted to recruit new members.

SMALL BOATS: A REPRESENTATIVE SAMPLING

Here is an illustrated gallery of some of the most popular class boats in the United States, accompanied by details of their size and sailing characteristics. But remember, for every boat pictured here, there are dozens of others which offer excitement and fun to any sailor.

Y-Flyer. Has many fleets in Midwest and in Canada, is baby cousin of Class A Scow. She is 18 feet over-all, is in the low-priced field. Counts about 2,000 boats in fast-growing class.

Lightning. With over 11,000 in class, this is one of the more popular sailboats in U.S. She is 19 feet long, ideal for racing, loafing; is in the medium price range.

Star. Measures 22 feet 8½ inches, is truly an international racer (active fleets on five continents). She is medium-priced, is hauled out, kept bone-dry between races.

Penguin. A tiny, 11½-foot centerboarder adapted to shallow bays and ponds. About 8,000 are scattered around country. Low-priced, Penguins are perfect for children, yet offer exciting small boat sailing to adults.

18

5-0-5. A high-performance two-man centerboard boat with a worldwide class organization. With a light hull (280 pounds), trapeze, and sophisticated rig, she is capable of exceptional speeds, both on and off the wind. Medium-priced.

Snipe. A trim 15 feet, 6 inches over-all, with a 5-foot beam and 20-foot, 3-inch mast. She draws 40 inches with daggerboard down, has two sails, main and jib, with a relatively small area (up to 115 square feet), which makes her an easy boat to handle. For racing she takes a skipper and one crew. Costs range from very inexpensive kits to modestly priced ready-to-sail. With thousands of boats registered around the world, the Snipe is one of the most popular two-man boats.

Sunfish. Introduced a totally new concept of small-boat design and has rapidly become the most popular sailboat in the U.S. with over 55,000 built. A very light, fully bouyant hull and a single sail make her an ideal boat for the beginner, yet her strict one-design characteristics and lively performance have made her a very popular single-handed racer. Easily beached and transported car-top.

Day Sailor. Popular, easily trailed 17-foot family boat with small cabin. Centerboard makes her ideal for coastal and inland waters. Planing hull and spinnaker give her good performance. Over 4,500 sailing in U.S.

420. A truly international class with over 20,000 boats around the world. Very light, planing hull gives the *420* fast, nimble performance. Spinnaker and small size (14 feet) make the boat an excellent junior trainer. Tight one-design rules.

International Tempest. Exceptionally high-performance, two-man racing keelboat currently enjoying Olympic status. Powerful sail plan combined with 22-foot easily driven fiberglass hull give her dinghy-like performance with the stability of a keelboat. She carries a spinnaker, has a retractable keel and rudder for trailing and is medium-priced.

24

Soling. A three-man Olympic keelboat, 27 feet long, with a fiberglass hull. Keen competition is enjoyed by skippers of this class, and strong fleets have developed in most areas of the U.S. Continual development of rig and hardware has resulted in a highly refined racing craft, yet one that is easy and fun to sail.

Flying Dutchman. One of the more popular planing hulls is the Flying Dutchman, a European design that has received a terrific boost from its Olympic status. The Dutchman's hull is built in either molded plywood or fiber glass and will readily plane in winds of over 10 knots. Her cockpit is designed to provide a highly efficient working area for both skipper and crew. A narrow, light displacement boat, the Dutchman requires a trapeze and over the years has developed into a highly sophisticated racing machine that will reward an experienced skipper and crew with a breath-taking ride.

Hobie Cat. An exciting new class of the increasingly popular catamaran design. Light, easily driven twin hulls and a powerful full-battened mainsail combine to give the craft exceptional speed, particularly reaching. Hobie Cat's deep V-shaped hulls eliminate need for centerboards and upturned bows allow boat to be sailed in heavy seas. In fact, many West Coast skippers frequently sail the cat in the surf, one of the more exhilarating sailing experiences. Relatively inexpensive.

2
Sailing
to Windward

FOR many of the million or more small boat sailors in the United States, the Lightning typifies the many kinds of class boats whose fleets are the backbone of the nation's sailing. Essentially unchanged since Olin Stephens first designed it in 1938, the Lightning has a stable, roomy hull, a well-balanced sail plan (see photograph on page 16), which includes a large spinnaker, and a retractable centerboard, as opposed to a fixed keel, so she can be easily hauled from place to place on a trailer.

A boat like the Lightning offers the average yachtsman good competition and safe fun in one package. Because she is an excellent training vehicle, simple to rig, easy to sail and powerful in a breeze, the Lightning is the boat used to illustrate the basic techniques of rigging and sailing in Chapters 2 and 3. However, any class boat owner—beginner or expert—should find much of the instruction relevant to his own class.

TUNING THE MAST

The first problem with the Lightning or any other small boat of similar rig is to place the mast in approximate position for proper boat balance and to ensure that it will remain straight under the strain of sailing. Recommended sequence of steps below begins with tuning ashore, in which the jumper stays are set up. Next comes tuning at mooring and tuning under way. Then come the refinements of combination tuning, which are purely trial-and-error and may take considerable time, since adjustment in one stay often means compensating adjustments in other stays.

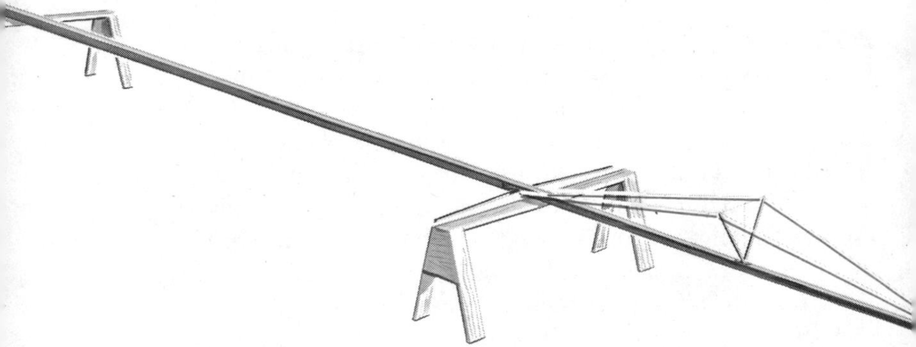

Figure 3. Tuning Ashore. Lay the mast so part under the jumper stays hangs free. Tighten the jumpers until the slack is removed. Be sure the tension on each jumper is the same. Jumper tension should be such that the mast bends back evenly from head to foot when the boat is rigged and slight backstay tension is applied.

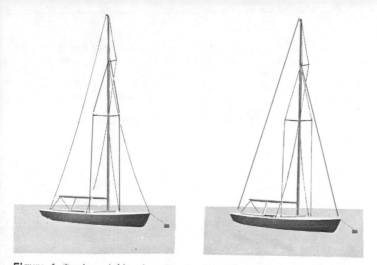

Figure 4. Tuning at Mooring. Start with all stays slack, then tighten the upper shrouds (above left, in blue) so the mast has equal clearance on each side of the deck opening. Next, adjust the jib-stay and the backstay (below right, in blue). Begin by moving the butt of the mast and setting the jibstay so that the mast just touches the rear edge of the deck opening when the top of the mast has 30 to 35 inches of rake (backward lean). Now tighten the backstay till the masthead begins bending back. Place wooden wedges at the foot of the mast and in the forward part of the deck opening.

Figure 5. Tuning Under Way. Tuning begins with both lower shrouds (below, in blue) hanging slightly slack. On the starboard tack (left) sight up the rear of the mast, which will probably be curved left or right. Pull inward on the starboard lower shroud. If the mast straightens, the lower shroud needs tightening. If the bend increases, pull inward on the upper starboard shroud. If the mast now straightens, the lower shroud needs loosening. Use the same procedure to tune the mast on the port tack (right) by adjusting the lower port shroud. Repeat the entire procedure until the mast is straight on both tacks.

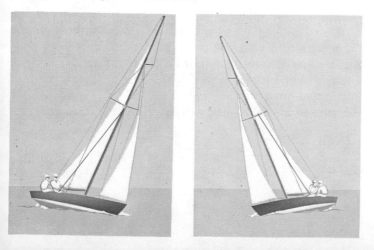

Combination tuning removes any remaining bends in the mast and puts as much tension as possible on the jibstay so that the jib will hold its proper shape. Use the backstay, upper and lower shrouds only. There is no set sequence. Start on one tack and straighten the most obvious bends first, working around to the minor bends. Then go onto the opposite tack and do the same. Repeat the cycle until the jibstay is taut and the mast stands straight on both tacks.

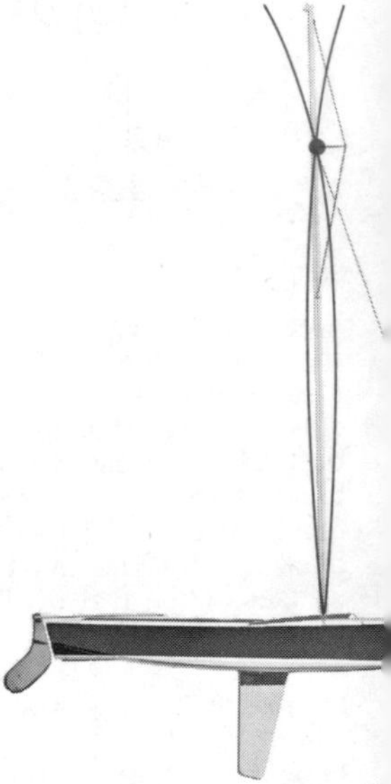

Figure 6. Tuning Errors. Errors resulting in forward or backward bowing of the mast (in blue) will reduce the effectiveness of the mainsail, designed for a straight mast. With the jibstay and upper shrouds taut, the point on the mast at the top of jibstay (blue dot) is held in a fixed position relative to the hull. When the masthead bends too far back, the mast below the blue dot bulges forward. Correct this by loosening the backstay, tightening the jumpers and lower shrouds. When the masthead bends forward, the mast below the dot bulges backward. The backstay must be tightened and the lower shrouds and jumpers loosened. Never correct a forward or backward bend with the jibstay or the upper shrouds.

THE FUNCTION OF FITTINGS

No two skippers will agree exactly on choice and location of fittings, but no small boat skipper questions the usefulness of the cam-action jam cleat (see circle, below). Pulling back and down secures any line in the jaws of the cleat, and pulling backward and up frees the line. In the recommended layout for principal fittings on a Lightning, the location of several useful cam cleats is indicated. Proper selection and installation of other fittings shown below is important. For strength, mainsheet blocks (1) are held to the deck with bolts, not screws. Jibsheet blocks (3) are lightweight for correct set of the jib in light weather. Spinnaker lead blocks (5) are set far out on the stern corners. Mooring fitting (8) is set close to the mast and far from the mooring chock (7) to keep the foredeck clear.

Figure 7. Fittings on a Lightning
(1) Mainsheet quarter block
(2) Mainsheet swivel cam cleat
(3) Jibsheet shackle and blocks
(4) Jibsheet cam-action cleat
(5) Spinnaker sheet lead block
(6) Spinnaker sheet cam cleat
(7) Mooring line chock
(8) Mooring line fitting

The spinnaker guy hook (see the circle below) and cam-action cleat permit rapid changes of the spinnaker trim. The hook allows the guy to keep the pole from rising out of control in strong winds.

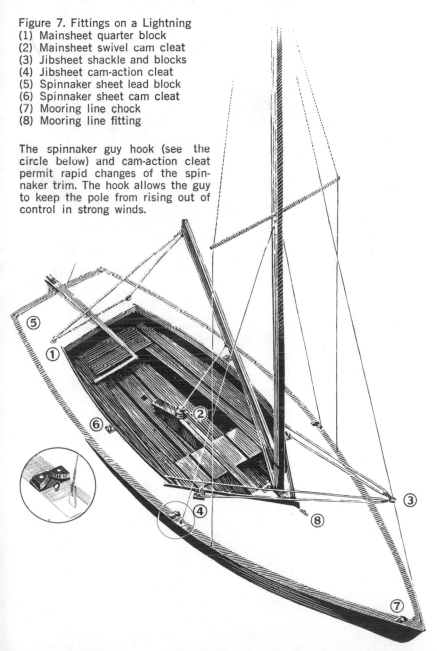

Figure 8. Chine Shape. Chine shape best for smooth flow of water past hull is a round rather than an angular shape. Rounding off the corner (see circle) of the chine up to radius of ½ inch is permitted by rules.

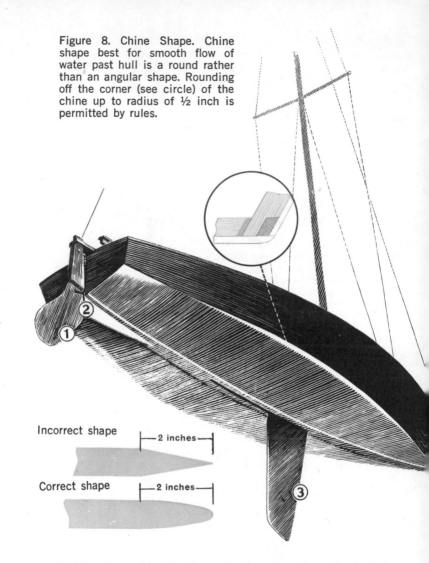

Incorrect shape

|—2 inches—|

Correct shape

|—2 inches—|

Rudder shape along the lower leading edge (1 on the hull drawing), should be streamlined the maximum allowable 2 inches. Many builders make a sharp V (see diagram above), which is inefficient at all times, and especially when the rudder is turned. Correct taper has an elliptical edge for a smoother flow while steering.

34

THE FUNCTION OF SHAPE

As water flows past under the hull, the shapes of the chine (page 34) and of the three vertical underwater appendages—the centerboard, the skeg and the rudder—have an effect on speed. In the Lightning class, within the limitations of the class rules, the best results come from the use of the shapes recommended here. The over-all shape of the hull itself is rigidly controlled by a published table of permissible variations from the class blueprint. Within the restrictions, the fastest hulls are those with flattest permissible run aft, narrowest beam and chines as high as permissible above water amidships.

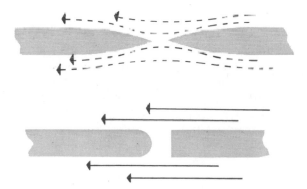

Figure 9. Skeg Shape. Skeg shape and shape of rudder (see 2 in Figure 8) should create straight lines of flow. Builders who taper skeg and rudder invite water flow to bend (broken arrows, above) and cause resistance. For straight lines of flow, the rudder should be as close to the skeg as possible and neither shape should be tapered (solid arrows, above).

(continued)

Figure 9 (continued). Centerboard Shape. Centerboard shape along leading edge (see 3 in Figure 8) may resemble either A or B (above) and produce good results. (The centerboard does not cut water head on, but at about a 5-degree angle of leeway.) Many builders deliver boards with the leading edge shaped as in C, where the legal 1-inch taper is an angular V. This is a poor shape. Always reshape the centerboard C to look like A or B by grinding away the metal (see portion of D, above). Legally, the width of the centerboard may be reduced up to ½ inch. For the trailing edge of the centerboard, a shape like B is best.

CONTROLLING THE ANGLE OF HEEL

The degree to which a boat heels, or tilts, determines the shape of its hull under water. Since the most desirable underwater shape depends on the speed of the boat, the crew must shift weight when the speed changes. In a light wind when speed is low, the resistance of the hull comes from friction between the hull and the water. To reduce resistance in a Lightning, the area of the hull under water is reduced by making the boat heel intentionally (see Figure 11A). At medium speed, the best shape results when the windward chine (where bottom joins topsides) is about 2 inches out of water (see Figure 11B). At high speed in strong winds, greatest resistance results because the boat makes waves. Keeping the boat as level as possible (see Figure 10) reduces wave formation and thus resistance. Arrow indicates wind direction.

Figure 10. A heavy breeze brings the crew out on the windward deck to hike, or lean out over water. In hard puffs skipper hikes also and purposely spills wind out of the mainsail to keep the boat from tipping over too far.

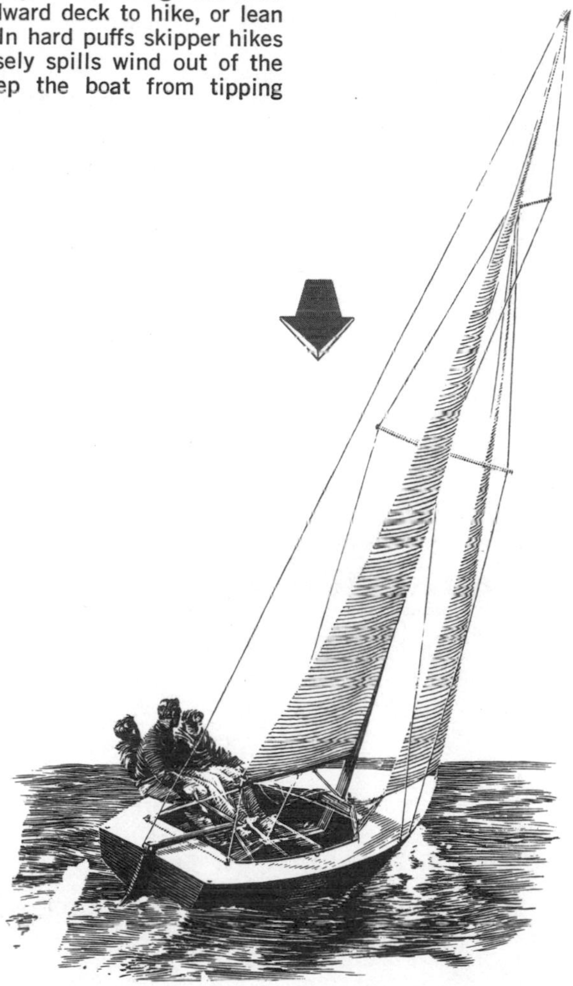

Figure 11

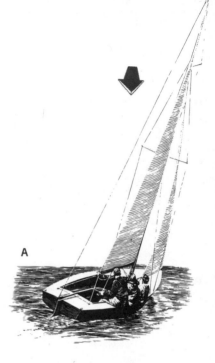

A

Figure 11A. A light breeze calls for the crew to sit on the leeward deck to make boat heel over as much as possible. The skipper makes use of the extension tiller so he, too, can get his weight well to leeward.

Figure 11B. A Medium breeze finds the crew on the windward side of the cockpit or divided between the sides of the boat, keeping the windward chine 2 inches off the water. The skipper sits to windward whenever possible.

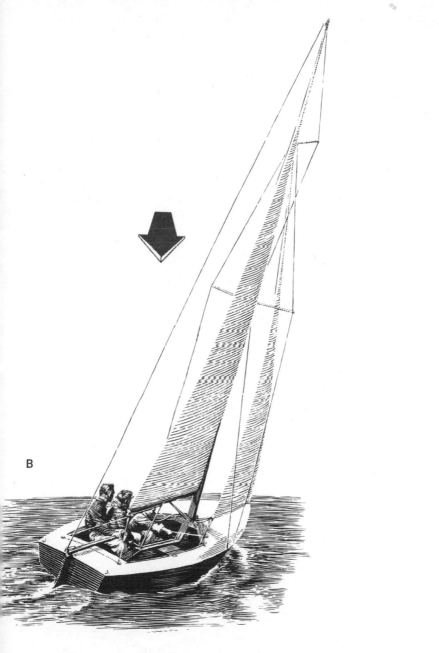

B

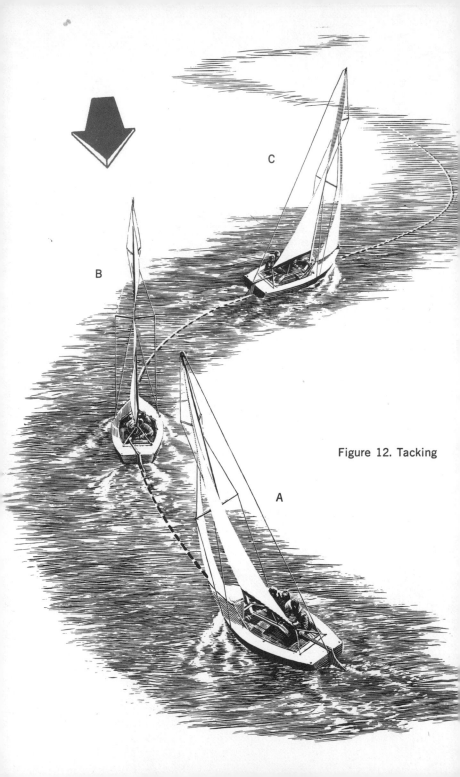

Figure 12. Tacking

GOING AGAINST THE WIND

No boat can sail directly into the wind, since the sails will not fill. However, a boat can arrive at a point directly upwind by making a series of diagonal moves, or tacks, first one way, then another (see Figure 13 on this page). Figure 12A–C shows the proper way to make the boat come about, that is, go from one tack to another. The skipper starts by pushing the tiller to leeward. As the boat turns into the wind, the crewman lets the jib sheet go, and the mainsail starts to move across the cockpit (see 12A). The critical moment comes when the boat is headed directly into the wind (see 12B). Wind no longer fills the sails. However, if the maneuver is carried out smoothly, the momentum of turn will carry the boat over onto the opposite tack. In 12C, the boat has moved successfully onto the new tack. The crew has fastened the jib on the lee side in position to form the important aerodynamic wind slot (see Figure 15, pages 44–45) between the jib and the mainsail.

Upwind sailing is done in a series of tacks made at an approximate 45-degree angle to the wind (Figure 13, below). This is as close to the wind direction as most centerboard boats can sail effectively. Surface ripples show

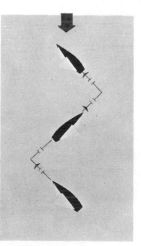

Figure 13. Tacking Upwind

the direction of the wind on the water, or true wind. On a moving hull, true wind is altered by the forward speed of the boat. This produces a slightly different wind direction, called the apparent wind. It lies between the true wind and the bow and is the force that actually drives the hull.

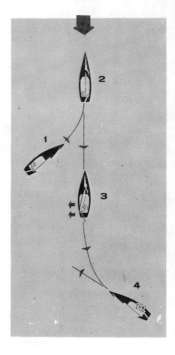

Figure 14. Getting Out of Irons

An upwind crisis (Figure 14) occurs when a boat (1) tries to come about but fails to complete the maneuver. The boat loses forward speed, stops (2), finally drifts backward out of control. This is called "getting in irons." To get out of the irons, the skipper pushes the tiller and the boom away from himself and holds them there (3). The stern soon swings to one side, the mainsail fills and the boat stops moving backward. At that point, the skipper pulls the tiller toward him (4) and the boat gains headway on a new tack. This maneuver can be hastened when the crew holds the jib to the side opposite the mainsail.

POWER FROM SAILS

When a boat is tacking upwind, two distinct forces combine to drive it ahead. First, as the wind strikes the windward side of the sail and is deflected along its curve, the wind exerts pressure on the sail and, because the sail is curved, part of this pressure acts in a forward direction to drive the boat ahead. The remaining pressure acts to push the boat sidewise, but this tendency is virtually nullified by the centerboard or keel, so that sidewise pressure is actually converted into heeling. Second, wind that slips along the lee side of the sail travels faster than wind on the windward side. Therefore a relative low-pressure area forms on the lee side which tends to suck the sail ahead, and with it the boat. This aerodynamic force actually provides more than twice as much forward drive as pressure on the windward side. On a boat with a jib, this force is very powerfully augmented by the presence of the slot effect (see Figure 15A and B). Resultant drive from all these sources makes the sailboat able to go faster diagonally into the wind than it will go downwind. In addition, the proper set and shape of the sails (see Figure 16) is vital in order to get the maximum driving power out of any given amount of wind filling the sails.

Sail shapes can either help or hinder the smooth flow of air along the surfaces of sail. Figure 16 shows five common shapes of mainsails.

Figure 15. The Slot Effect

A

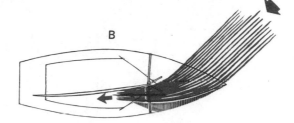

B

A slot effect occurs when the jib funnels air through the slot formed between the jib and the mainsail (see arrow in A, opposite, and overhead view of slot in B, above). Narrowness of the slot forces air to increase speed. This causes a strong low-pressure area on the lee side of the mainsail (by operation of Bernoulli's principle, any increase in airflow speed decreases internal pressure of the air at that point). This "vacuum" pulls the boat ahead and is an important factor in sail power.

C   D

Adjusting the slot by varying the jib's distance from the main-sail is done by tightening or loosening the jib sheet. Bringing the jib too close (see C, above) causes the wind to deflect into the mainsail. The mainsail then curves away from the jib. The slot becomes distorted and loses its effectiveness. The correct jib posi-tion (see D, above) smoothly funnels the wind parallel to the lee side of the mainsail. The jib should set slightly farther from the mainsail in a strong wind than in a light one. In racing, changing the length of the jib sheet by 2 inches or so can well make the difference between winning and losing.

45

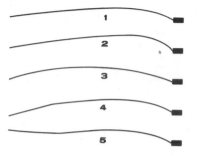

Figure 16. Sail Shapes. (1) The most desirable shape is a curve that flattens more and more toward leech. (2) Sail with too much curve forward is too easily backwinded by the jib. (3) A uniform curve, mistakenly shunned by many, is good in a light wind. (4) Sail with a tight leech is bad in a strong wind. (5) Loose leech is a poor shape in any wind.

SHAPING SAIL

Shaping mainsail. This will help increase power. For strong winds, flatten sail by pulling on the downhaul and the outhaul. (The blue line in Figure 17A indicates flattened curve.) For light winds, get a fuller curve by slacking off on the outhaul and the downhaul. (The blue line in Figure 17B indicates deepened curve.) Many classes now use a fixed boom and a Cunningham in lieu of a downhaul. The Cunningham is merely a grommet inserted approximately 12 inches up from the tack of the mainsail which when pulled down by a line acts like a downhaul, flattening the main.

Shaping the jib for greatest power. The primary consideration is that the jibstay remain very taut. The second factor is the proper location of jib-sheet leads on deck.

In the Lightning, correctly placed jib leads will hold the jib so that the entire length of jib luff will flutter at the same time when the boat swings into the wind. Viewed from above (see Figure 17C), the sheets extended through the leads to the bow should form an angle of 10 degrees or less with the centerline of the hull.

46

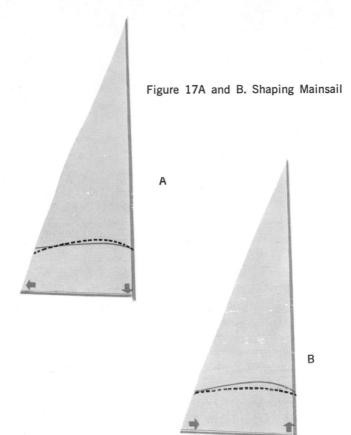

Figure 17A and B. Shaping Mainsail

A

B

Figure 17C. Proper Jib Angle

Figure 18

Shaping with sheet. The skipper should try to get a direct downpull on the leech of the mainsail to bring it into the plane formed by the mast and the boom. And for best performance, the boom should be kept as close to the centerline of the boat as possible. Since the standard mainsheet rig on Lightnings allows the boom to fall off to leeward (see Figure 18), most skippers use some sort of jamming device on the transom to lock the mainsheet and keep the boom on the centerline.

Shaping with the boom vang. This is the best way to keep mainsail leech straight during strong, puffy winds when mainsheet has to be slacked quickly from time to time to spill wind. Otherwise, the boom vang (see Figure 19) is seldom used in windward sailing, since the downward pull of the mainsheet will keep the leech straight enough. However, on courses across the wind and downwind, the boom vang should be in constant use to keep the leech straight and the boom under control, since, on these points of sailing, the boom hangs farther out and the mainsheet cannot pull hard enough to control the boom.

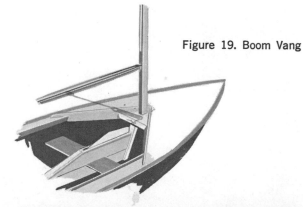

Figure 19. Boom Vang

BALANCE OF BOAT

When all wind and water forces affecting a sailboat are in proper balance and the boat is sailed at a 45-degree angle to true wind with the tiller held at dead center (Figure 21, page 51), the hull will travel forward in a straight line. If the tiller must be held to windward to keep the boat on a straight course at a 45-degree angle to the wind (see Figure 20B), the boat has weather helm; if the tiller must be held to leeward (see Figure 20A), the boat has lee helm. A boat with lee or weather helm is slowed down due to the continual drag of rudder, which must be held at an angle to keep the boat on course. In a race, weather helm should be corrected immediately (see page 52) or the boat will soon be passed by others. Lee helm is serious even for noncompetitive sailors because the boat will be reluctant to head up safely in a strong puff. Although in a properly balanced boat the rudder is amidships when a boat sails a straight course, the rudder should transmit a slight leeward pull to the tiller. This shows the rudder is helping the centerboard resist leeward drift. When the tiller does not have leeward pull and feels dead in the skipper's hand, the boat is not properly balanced, and correction as if for a slight leeward helm (see page 55) should be made.

CORRECTING WEATHER HELM

In heavy weather, all conventional sailing craft create a large leeward bow wave, which pushes the bow to windward and causes a temporary weather helm. One way to correct this is to move the crew farther back in the cockpit (see Figure 22), bringing the forward part of the boat

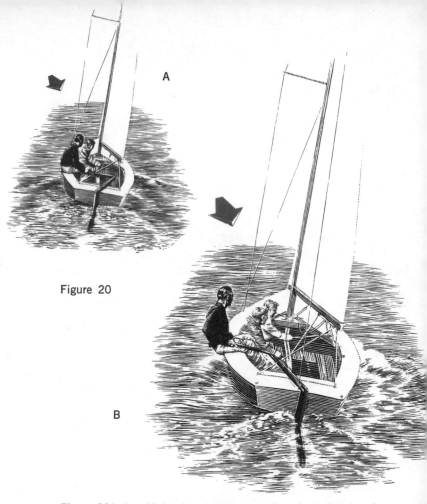

A

Figure 20

B

Figure 20A. Lee Helm. Lee helm occurs in a boat that heads away from the wind when the tiller is held amidships. To stay on course, the tiller must be put to leeward.

Figure 20B. Weather Helm. Weather helm occurs in a boat that tends to head into the wind when the tiller is held amidships, so the tiller has to be held to windward.

Figure 21. Proper helm keeps the boat on course with the rudder amidships. Ideally, there should be slight pressure wanting to swing the tiller to leeward.

Figure 21. Proper Helm

Figure 22

out of the water (see arrows in Figure 22) and reducing the bow wave. Do not use this technique in milder weather to correct weather helm but apply one of the remedies for permanent weather helm which follow.

Figure 23. Correcting Weather Helm (1). The first remedy for permanent weather helm is to lift the centerboard a few inches. The most effective remedy of all is to reduce the rake of the mast, then retune the entire rig.

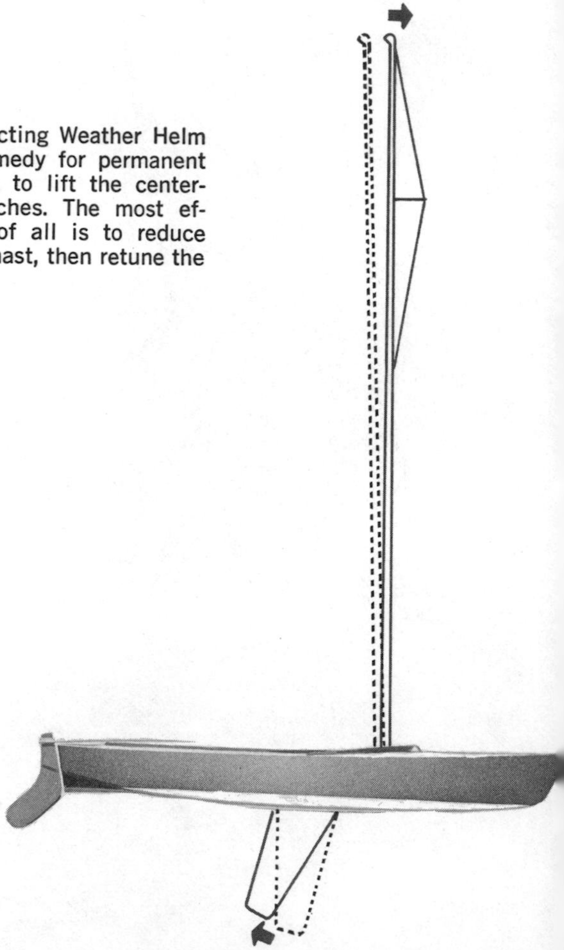

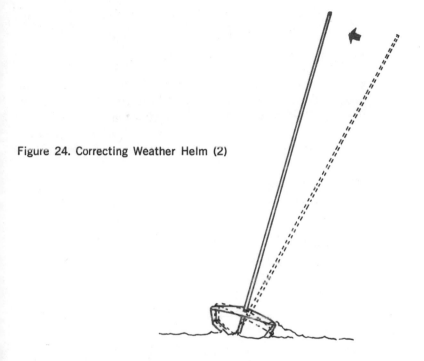

Figure 24. Correcting Weather Helm (2)

Correcting by Balancing. (See Figure 24.) Keep the boat as level as possible, since a level boat makes a smaller leeward bow wave. By keeping the boat on an even keel, you will also bring the center of effort (point in sail plan where the force of wind is theoretically concentrated) more nearly over the center of lateral resistance (point under the hull where the total force resisting drift is theoretically located). This means less weather helm.

Figure 25. Correcting Weather Helm (3)

Correcting by Trimming. (See Figure 25.) This can be accomplished by easing the mainsheet or trimming the jib —or both. Even though these adjustments may interfere with the best setting of sails at a given moment, the boat will, nevertheless, perform better, since weather helm causes greater loss of speed than badly trimmed sails. In a heavy wind, easing the mainsheet gives far better results than trimming the jib.

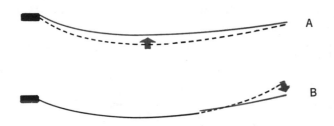

Figure 26. Correcting Weather Helm (4)

Correcting by Shaping the Mainsail. (See Figure 26.) This can be done simply by flattening the curve of the mainsail (see A, above). A tight leech may also cause weather helm. Stretching the leech by hand may produce a flatter curve aft (see B, above). However, a leech tight enough to cause a permanent weather helm will probably have to be resewn by a sailmaker.

CORRECTING LEE HELM

Since lee helm is opposite to weather helm in every respect, corrective measures are opposite. The preferred method is to increase the rake in the mast and then retune the rig. Other remedies for lee helm are to move the crew forward, ease the jib sheet, pull in the mainsail, make the mainsail take a fuller curve by slacking outhaul and down-haul, or lower the centerboard. For maximum centerboard correction, the top edges of the centerboard trunk can be notched to let the centerboard swing as far forward as class rules will allow.

Lee helm in moderate and heavy conditions is particu-larly dangerous because the boat bears off in hard puffs when, for safety's sake, the skipper is trying to head the boat into the wind to spill wind from the sails. The problem is particularly acute with centerboard boats, which lack the stability afforded by the heavy ballast of a metal keel.

HIKING TO WINDWARD

The most strenuous part of class boat sailing comes when heavy winds heel the boat so that more of the bottom than usual comes out of the water (see the photograph on page 19). To counteract heeling, the crew hikes, hanging almost entirely out of the boat, held in only by hiking straps (see Figure 27). The skipper does his part in hiking, at the same time steering with the very end of the tiller extension to head the boat into the wind. When a sudden puff strikes, he eases the mainsheet to spill some of the wind safely out of the mainsail, and all hands should hike even farther, moving quickly, since every second saved in bringing the boat back to proper sailing angle means gaining on competitors, as well as being in a safer and more comfortable sailing position. Peaks of action like this make sailing men love the sport.

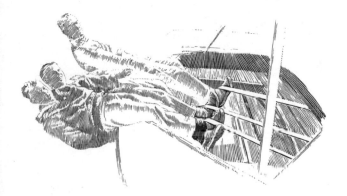

Figure 27. Hiking

3

Sailing to Leeward

IN this section the question of getting downwind with maximum speed is discussed. Primarily, this means sailing much of the time with a spinnaker billowing out over the bow. It also means extra watchfulness on the part of the crew. The spinnaker is a tricky, powerful sail that must be handled with respect. But it can also be a lot of fun. Properly set in a good wind, the spinnaker can provide the most exciting ride of the day. However, proper setting requires skill, coordination and fast action. On the following pages the two most difficult maneuvers with a spinnaker—setting and jibing—are described step by step.

SETTING THE SPINNAKER

The spinnaker is not fastened along one of its edges to a stay or to the mast as are other sails. Instead, it floats free in the breeze, a spherical triangle held only at the corners. The head, or upper corner, is held aloft by the spinnaker halyard, which serves to raise the spinnaker. The tack (the lower corner next to the spinnaker pole) is attached to one end of the spinnaker guy. The clew (the other lower corner) is held by one end of the spinnaker sheet. In hoisting, the preferred method consists of a series

Figure 28A. Spinnaker Ready. The spinnaker ready to hoist (in the box) is prepared first by leading the guy (1) through the lead block (2) and attaching to the spinnaker tack (3); second, by snapping the pole fitting (4) onto the guy, raising the pole with the topping lift (5) and attaching the pole to the fitting (6) on the mast; third, by leading the sheet (7) through the lead block (8) and attaching the sheet to the spinnaker clew (9); and last, by running the halyard (10) outside the jib and attaching the halyard to the head of the spinnaker (11).

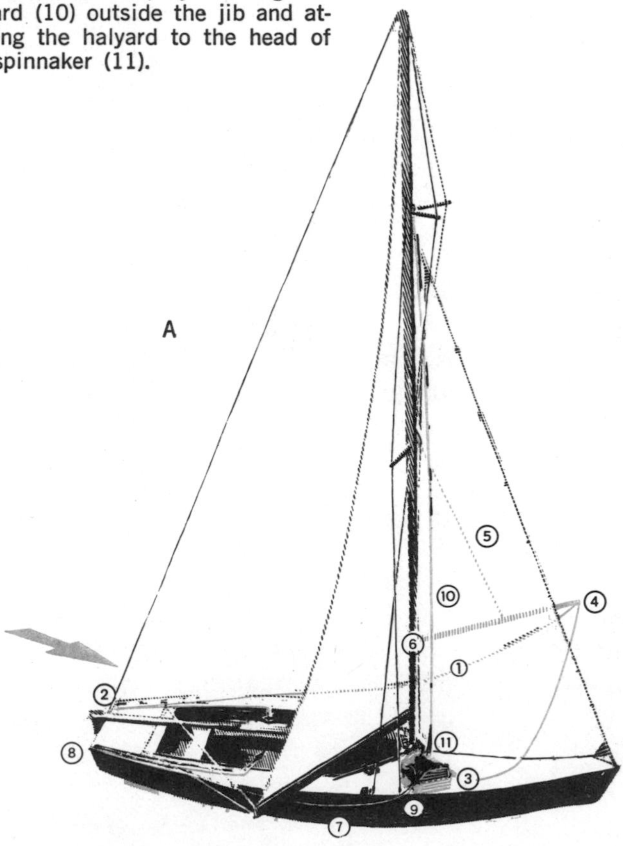

of actions performed in rapid succession in such a way that no one has to leave the cockpit. (Putting a man on the foredeck makes the boat easy to tip and slows it down.) The division of duties among the men depends on the ability of each. The first phase, getting ready (see Figure

Figure 28B. Hoisting the Spinnaker. The halyard pulls the sail up the mast while the sail hangs limp in the lee of the mainsail. The sheet pulls the clew aft momentarily to prevent the sail from twisting. The guy is pulled through the pole fitting to bring the tack toward the end of the pole.

(continued)

B

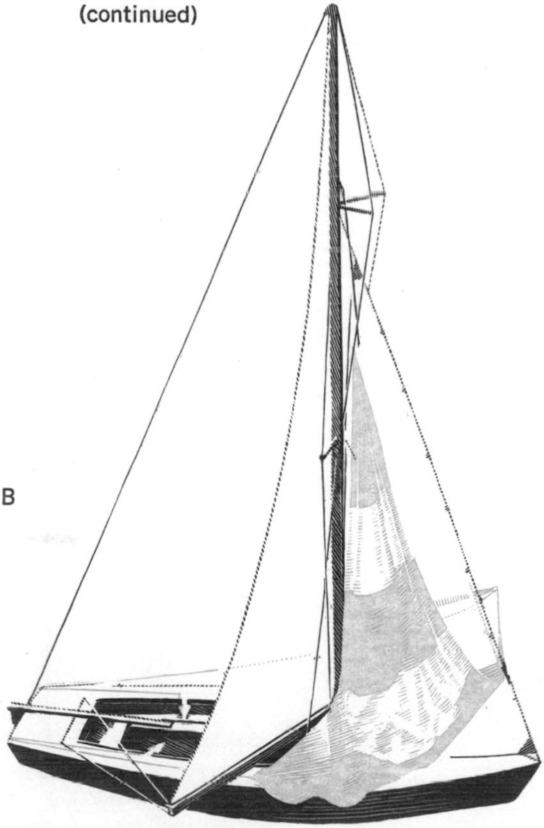

28A), is completed before reaching the mark that begins the leeward leg. Hoisting the spinnaker in the lee of the mainsail where there is relatively little wind (see Figure 28B) starts as the boat rounds the mark. Then, as the spinnaker fills, the jib is dropped (Figure 28C). A well-drilled crew will have the spinnaker flying within 10 seconds after the mark is turned.

Figure 28C. Spinnaker Filling. The guy has pulled the tack to the end of the pole, drawn the pole astern, been hooked on the deck and cleated. The jib is dropped onto the deck as the spinnaker fills. The spinnaker will set properly when the sheet is eased and the lower corners are made level.

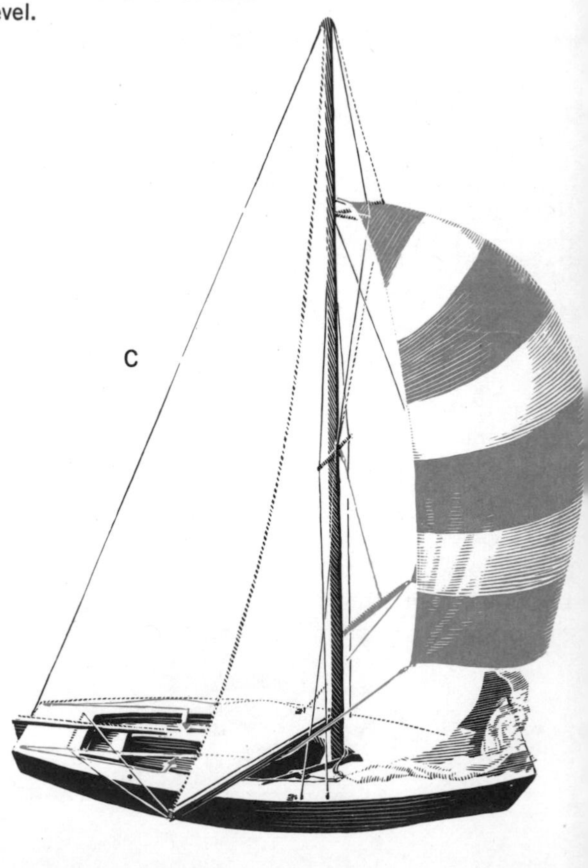

C

Figure 29. Fittings at each end of the spinnaker pole are hooked to the mast and around the spinnaker guy (A). The guy runs freely, so the sail can be raised or lowered in the lee of the mainsail without anyone's having to go on deck.

The box (B) (or turtle as it is sometimes called) can be either heavy cardboard (carry a spare) or an inexpensive plastic laundry basket, notched with three narrow V-shaped slots. The lower corners of the sail are first wedged into notches and the sail is then folded into turtle from the foot of the sail up, without twisting. The head is put in the last notch.

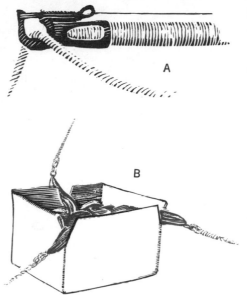

JIBING: THE MODERN, SAFE TECHNIQUE

Sailing to leeward, the skipper must always steer so that the wind comes from the corner of the stern opposite the mainsail (see arrows, Figure 30). If the skipper wishes to set a new downwind course which shifts the wind to the other corner of the stern, then the position of the mainsail must be reversed (or jibed). Since the spinnaker pole must always be kept on the side opposite the mainsail, the spinnaker must be jibed simultaneously. Jibing is the most difficult and dangerous maneuver in sailing. Close attention to the method described on pages 64–67 will make safe jibing relatively easy. This method keeps all the men in the cockpit so that the stability of the boat, always precarious in jibing, will be kept at a maximum throughout the maneuver. In general, the helmsman handles the mainsail, the middle crewman is responsible for keeping the spinnaker at right angles to the wind while the boat turns beneath the sail, and the forward crewman or spin-

Figure 30A. Ready to Jibe. The skipper steers with his knees, pulls back on the mainsheet to make room for the spinnaker man to face aft and squeeze forward of the boom vang to reach the end of the spinnaker pole up on the mast. The middle crewman, having released the guy from the deck hook, holds both the guy and the sheet.

A

naker man is responsible for shifting the spinnaker pole (and with it the spinnaker) from one side across to the other side.

Figure 30B. Beginning the Jibe. The skipper swings the tiller to bear off and pulls the mainsheet rapidly in. The spinnaker man removes the pole from the mast and snaps the sheet into the pole fitting, while the middle crewman slacks the sheet and trims the guy to keep the spinnaker full and at right angles to the wind.

(continued)

B

C

Figure 30C. Halfway in the Jibe. The men duck as the wind swings the mainsail rapidly across the cockpit. The skipper momentarily shifts the tiller in the opposite direction. The spinnaker man pulls the trip line to free the left corner of the spinnaker from the left end of the pole and moves the pole to the right.

66

Figure 30D. Completed Jibe. The jibe is complete when the spinnaker man snaps the left end of the pole to the mast and the
skipper lets the mainsail all the way out on the port side. By
then the skipper has the tiller in his left hand and takes the
strain of what is now the guy in his right, so the middle crewman
can hook the guy to the deck.

Figure 31. Beam-reaching

CARRYING THE SPINNAKER ACROSS THE WIND

The usefulness of the spinnaker is not limited to sailing directly or almost directly with the wind (see Figure 30A, page 64). The spinnaker can be carried diagonally downwind (broad-reaching) or at right angles to wind (beam-reaching), as in Figure 31. Since it is more powerful than a jib, the spinnaker is flown whenever possible in racing. (However, carrying the spinnaker closer to the wind than about 90 degrees causes it to collapse.) On a reach, the pull of the spinnaker is sidewise and can tip the boat over if it is allowed to heel too far. The skipper should watch for strong puffs and bear off more downwind, so when the puff reaches the boat the spinnaker will be pulling more forward, the direction in which the boat has the greatest stability. Once the boat heels too far with its spinnaker flying, the hull develops such weather helm that bearing off is impossible. Then the sheet must be let out quickly and the spinnaker collapsed to bring the boat back toward an even keel.

4
Sailing a Planing Hull

THE 5-0-5 hull at left, surging ahead like a surfboard, is one of an exciting type of sailing craft called planing boats. Capable of moving at triple the speed of conventional boats, they have advanced the art of sailing into a truly new dimension. Until planing boats were developed, the speed of a sailboat was limited by the length of its waterline. Every boat moving through the water made a bow wave and a stern wave (see Figure 32A). And once the boat reached a given speed, it could not go any faster, because to do so it would have had to climb up its bow wave. Because of its weight and the shape of the bottom, the conventional displacement hull could not rise out of its own wave trap. The planing boat, however, is designed to escape that trap. Light in weight, with powerful sails and a flat stern, it behaves like a displacement boat

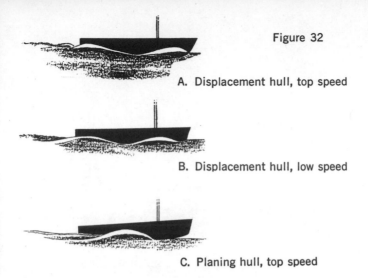

Figure 32

A. Displacement hull, top speed

B. Displacement hull, low speed

C. Planing hull, top speed

in light winds (see Figure 32B). But when a puff hits, the force of the wind, counterbalanced by the weight of the crew, pushes the boat onto the bow wave. Then the flat bottom, instead of mushing down in the water, forces the light hull toward the surface until it pops out of the trap and skims along (Figure 32C) on the crest of its own bow wave.

On the following pages, Mark and Sally Lindsay, top Eastern husband-and-wife 5-0-5 sailors, demonstrate skills for both planing sailors who want to master their high art and for sailors of conventional hulls who can use some of these same advanced techniques to make their own boats go faster.

SPECIAL GEAR FOR PLANING

The 5-0-5 carries all the equipment and has the design characteristics commonly found in planing boats. She has a

72

flat stern to help her get onto a plane. She weighs 280 pounds (compared to 381 for a comparable nonplaning class, the Snipe) and has 172 square feet of sail in her mainsail and jib (a Snipe has 115). Because of her light weight and her large sail area, she needs special gear to keep her upright. The most potent piece of equipment is the trapeze (1 in Figure 33). This consists of a wire attached to the upper part of the mast, with a wide belt or harness that snaps on at the lower end. In heavy winds the crewman clips the belt to the wire and hangs out over the windward side (see Figure 39B). There he can exert three times the leverage of a man perched on the windward rail. The less spectacular hiking straps (2) are canvas belts under which the legs can be hooked to allow both the skipper and the crew to hike. The tiller extension (3) lets the skipper control the boat while he is hiking. The boom vang (4) is a short wire that holds the mainsail in

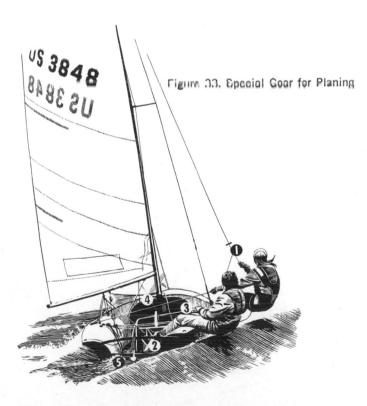

Figure 33. Special Gear for Planing

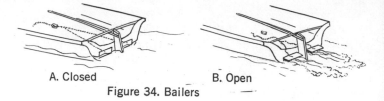

A. Closed   B. Open

Figure 34. Bailers

its best shape offwind. The trapdoor bailers (5) are a pair of hinged flaps held by elastic cord (Figure 34A) that can be released (Figure 34B) to drain the fast-moving hull if she ships water.

TAMING THE TRAPEZE

The trapeze is used only when wind is blowing so hard that hiking will not keep the hull flat. Crew, however, wears harness continuously, whether it is attached to wire or not. The wire—actually two wires, one on each side of the mast—is held secure at the lower end by an elastic cord. Getting out over the water is fast, tricky work. In Figure 35, the crew shows the proper procedure.

Figure 35. Taming the Trapeze

A

The trapeze is used when the wind is blowing so hard that normal hiking will not keep the hull flat. Crew, however, wears harness continuously, whether it is attached to wire or not. The wire—actually two wires, one on each side of the mast—is secured at the lower end by shock (elastic) cord. Getting out over the water is fast, tricky work. Here, Sally Lindsay shows the proper procedure. First (A), with the jib sheet in the left hand and the wire in the right, she removes left foot from under hiking strap, then (B) brings the leg up to brace against gunwale near shroud. At the same time, the jib sheet is cleated and the trapeze wire is held to maintain balance.

(continued)

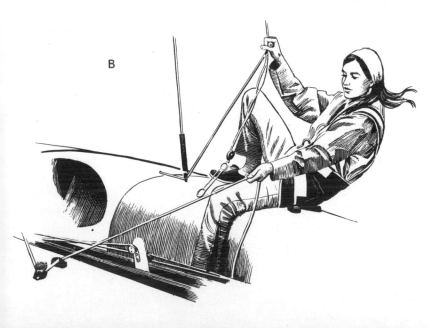

B

Figure 35 (continued). Sally then uses her left hand and right leg to push away from hull (C), at the same time hanging from the trapeze wire with right hand. Once out over the water, the left hand is used to fasten trapeze wire to hook on harness (D) and the right arm is relaxed, shifting weight totally to harness. Now completely out over water in perfect horizontal position (E), Sally uses both hands to further trim the jib sheet. Notice the right (forward) leg is stiff, the left (aft) leg is flexed to act as shock absorber. Coming back in is very much the reverse of getting out.

E

GETTING THE BOAT TO PLANE

Getting a boat to plane is fun in any circumstances, but in a race it is absolutely essential, for the first boat up will double the speed of its rivals. Therefore the skipper and his crew must watch the wind and learn to feel when the boat is going almost fast enough. In a 5-0-5 this will be at about 6 knots and requires a wind of at least 10 knots. The instant they feel conditions are right, the men must lean far out, pump the sails and try to bounce the boat out of the trough created by its bow and stern waves and get it up onto a plane.

Figure 36. Getting the Boat to Plane

A

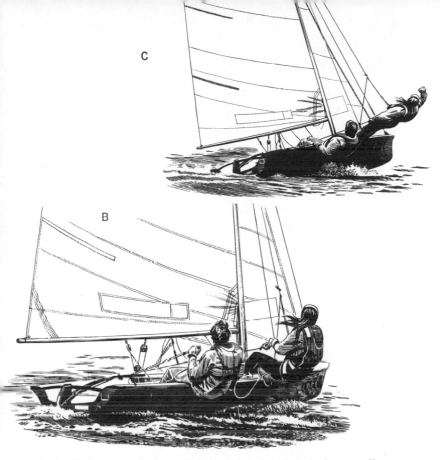

A. Ready to plane, Mark and Sally are poised, ready for a puff to hit. Wind is broadside. Sally holds the jib sheet and is partially out on trapeze. Mark holds the mainsheet while watching for a dark patch on the water indicating an approaching puff.

B. The wind hits and the boat accelerates. Both skipper and crew quickly move farther outboard. At the same time, Mark slacks the mainsheet slightly, ready to pull it in fast to help pump the boat onto a plane.

C. Breaking onto a plane, Mark trims the main quickly and both move far outboard, demonstrating top hiking and trapeze form. The boat now surges ahead on top of its own bow wave, leaving a typical flat wake as the 5-0-5 jumps speed from 6 knots to 10 or more.

The most important factor in planing, as in all sailing, is the direction and strength of the wind. A planing boat reacts most efficiently to wind coming in from slightly forward of broadside. Therefore, in Figure 36 the skipper and crew bring the 5-0-5 broadside to the wind. As a puff hits, they do a precisely timed, simultaneous backward and outward hike to keep the boat on its feet so its broad stern can help lift it up. On a gusty day, when the wind first drops below planing strength and then rises again quickly, the 5-0-5 will go on and off plane repeatedly. The skipper and crew then have to move in and out constantly to keep the hull flat on the water. If they move out too soon, the boat will tip awkwardly to windward, spilling wind from the sails and losing way. And if they move out too late, the boat will miss the chance to get up; or at worst it will flip over, leaving all hands paddling in the water.

STAYING ON A PLANE

Once the boat is on a plane, keeping it there calls for finesse and judgment, especially in maintaining the best, most powerful angle with the wind. As any boat accelerates, the direction of the wind experienced on board shifts toward the bow (small arrows in Figure 37), even though the direction of true wind over the water (heavy arrow) remains the same. This new and varying wind direction, or apparent wind—a combination of the true wind and the air which naturally flows back as the boat moves rapidly forward—will eventually swing so far toward the bow that the boat will slow down and drop off its plane if it is not handled properly. Therefore, as the boat accelerates, the skipper keeps the apparent wind at the correct angle by driving off (veering downwind).

Figures 38A, B and C show how the skipper keeps the apparent wind coming over the side of the hull at a con-

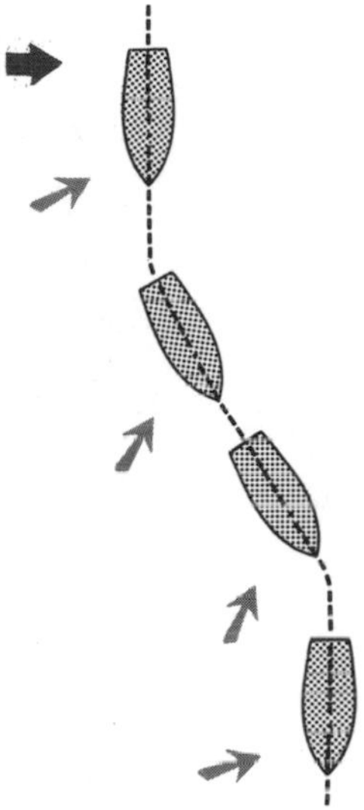

Figure 37. The Apparent Wind. The apparent wind shifts forward and then back, forcing the boat to drive off and then return to its original course.

stant angle. As the boat speeds up, both men have to hike out farther. For not only does the apparent wind change direction, but the increasing speed of the boat itself adds to the power of the apparent wind. When the wind drops off, however, the skipper must sense the change immediately and swing the boat back to the original course. The snakelike path that results from driving off and coming back is typical of a well-skippered planing hull. The enormous advantage of keeping the boat driving at top speed more than makes up for the curving passage through the water.

A. In a steady wind, the boat planes perfectly, kept flat by the Lindsays' hiking.
B. In a rising wind, Mark drives (veers) off and slacks main. Both hike out farther.
C. With the boat again flat in the water and under control, Mark pumps the main to add speed as he continues to drive the hull off.

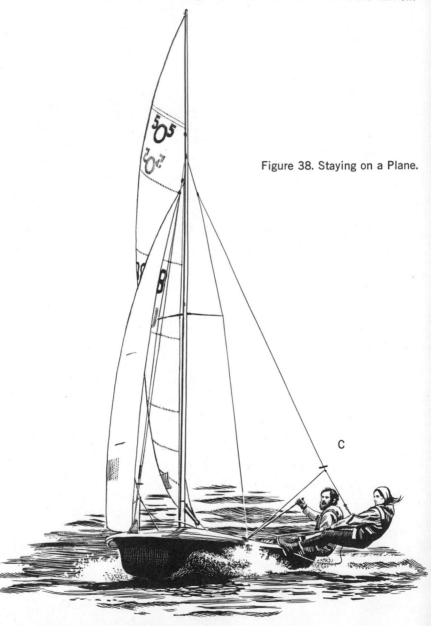

Figure 38. Staying on a Plane.

5
Off the Wind in a Planing Hull

RIDING THE WAVES

ONCE a skipper and crew have mastered the technique and timing of planing their boat, they are ready to ride the waves, an advanced maneuver used to get optimum speed in downwind sailing.

In the lakes and bays where planing boats usually are sailed, the waves tend to be short and choppy. Unfortunately, these are the hardest to ride, since they lack power and hence cannot carry the boat any great distance or lift its speed more than 3 or 4 mph. Nevertheless, each wave, if ridden properly, can mean a gain of a few yards; and over the full course of a race, these yards can add up to victory. A good skipper must be skillful at handling a boat in a choppy sea. As each wave approaches, he catches

Figure 39. Riding the Waves

A. As a wave approaches from the right, Mark pulls the tiller to start the stern swinging into the crest.

B. With the boat's stern toward the swell, the Lindsays slack the sails, begin to hike out.

C. When the crest reaches the middle of the hull, the sails are trimmed sharply to help the boat accelerate.

the crest, holds it for a moment, then drops off again, ready for the next one. So quickly do skipper and crew manipulate the tiller and sails that the entire sequence shown in Figure 39 takes no more than 10 seconds.

In a larger sea with more carrying power, the jobs of both the skipper and crew are much easier. The sequence can last for half a minute or more; and if the wind is blowing hard enough, a well-balanced boat can hold onto a crest for nearly a quarter of a mile, skidding down the face of the wave at 15 to 20 mph. A planing ride at these speeds is unlike anything else in small boat sailing. A flat wake hisses out astern as the boat surges forward with such steady power that she seems to be riding on steel rails. One false swing of the tiller, however, and this exhilarating charge downwind can come to a sudden, wet halt.

Waves from the Side. The first move in riding waves that come from the side (see Figure 40) is an abrupt turn to swing the broad stern of the boat into the crest. When the wave hits, the stern rises and the hull gathers speed as it starts to run down the front of the swell. To stay on the wave as long as possible, pump the sails in hard, hike, or get out in the trapeze if the wind is blowing hard enough.

Figure 40. Riding Waves. The boat turns approximately 20 degrees off course in order to catch the swells.

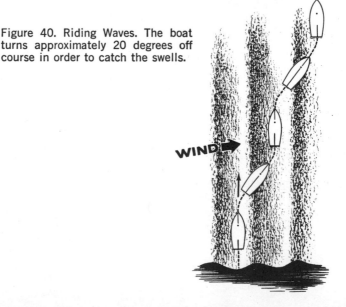

WIND

Waves from the Stern. When the swells are coming in from behind, there is no need to make a violent change of course since both the boat and the wave system are going in the same general direction. However, when the first crest moves under the boat, the skipper should turn slightly off course in a gentle, even curve to keep the wind flowing into the sails at the best angle. Veering off like this also prolongs the ride by sending the hull slanting across the face of the wave rather than straight down it.

Although the maneuvering of the boat in this situation is comparatively simple, the men aboard must be careful to keep their weight directly over the crest so the boat balances properly throughout the ride. This means they must slide forward and then backward inside the cockpit as the wave surges past. The movements of both crewmen must be smooth and steady, and their timing precise. Otherwise, the boat will wobble down into the trough, losing as much as 50 per cent of its speed—and perhaps a race.

Figure 41. Planing with a Spinnaker

PLANING WITH A SPINNAKER

As we learned in Chapter 3, the spinnaker is a powerful, full-bellied sail. Sailors of heavier conventional boats use spinnakers on virtually all downwind runs; but planing skippers use them less often for two reasons. First, the sail is so big that it can overpower a sensitive boat like the 5-0-5 when the wind freshens. Second, by tacking downwind, catching the waves and keeping the boat planing, a skipper can often reach the finish line faster sailing under jib and main than he would sailing a straight course under a spinnaker. In light and medium winds, however, one must set the big sail to keep the boat moving. And in very light air, one must pump the spinnaker to get the boat up onto the surface where it can plane.

Flying the spinnaker from the trapeze is thrilling but tricky business. The crew must simultaneously keep the boat flat and the spinnaker properly set. Here Sally quickly trims the chute and Mark veers off as a puff hits. Notice the jib is left flying, generally the case in all except very light air, when it is rolled up on its own luff wire by means of a roller-furling device.

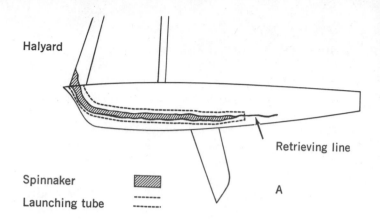

Halyard

Retrieving line

Spinnaker

Launching tube

A

Figure 42. The Spinnaker Launcher. The technique of setting the spinnaker on a boat such as the 5-0-5, Flying Dutchman, or Fireball has been changed from the more traditional method described in Chapter 3 with the advent of the spinnaker launching tube (A, above), a long underdeck socklike device attached to an opening in the bow of the boat (B, below), which holds the spinnaker when not in use. All lines are left attached; to hoist, one merely pulls the chute out of the tube with the halyard. To drop the chute, the spinnaker guy, sheet and halyard are released and the sail is pulled back into the tube by a line attached to the center of the sail (see 1, Figure 41). A remarkably quick and effective device, the spinnaker repeatedly can be raised or lowered without the crew's ever having to touch it, concentrating instead on the placement of the pole and the trimming of the sail.

B

SAILING OUT OF A CAPSIZE

No matter how good he is, sooner or later anyone who goes out in a sailboat turns over. But in a planing hull, a capsize does not mean the end of the race. Practically all planing boats have built-in flotation tanks, and since the hulls weigh so little, they float high in the water, even when swamped. If the crewmen learn to move fast enough, they can get their craft upright without dropping too far behind in the fleet. As water pours into the cockpit the skipper and crew scramble to the high side to keep the mast from going under. Then they quickly pull the boat back on her feet, trim the sails and, with bailers open, have the 5-0-5 up and planing less than 30 seconds after she went over.